YEMEN

...in Pictures

Visual Geography Series®

YEMEN

...in Pictures

Prepared by
Geography Department

Lerner Publications Company
Minneapolis

Independent Picture Service

A Yemeni fisherman displays his catch.

This book is a newly commissioned title in the Visual Geography Series. The text is set in 10/12 Century Textbook.

LIBRARY OF CONGRESS CATALOGING-IN-PUBLICATION DATA

Yemen in Pictures / prepared by Geography Department, Lerner Publications Company.
  p. cm — (Visual geography series)
  Includes index.
  Summary: Describes the topography, history, society, economy, and governmental structure of Yemen.
  ISBN 0-8225-1911-9 (lib. bdg.)
  1. Yemen. [1. Yemen.] I. Lerner Publications Company. Geography Dept. II. Series: Visual geography series (Minneapolis, Minn.)
DS247.Y453 1993   93-3178
953.3—dc20   CIP
                                              AC

International Standard Book Number: 0-8225-1911-9
Library of Congress Catalog Card Number: 93-3178

VISUAL GEOGRAPHY SERIES®

Publisher
Harry Jonas Lerner
Senior Editor
Mary M. Rodgers
Editors
Gretchen Bratvold
Tom Streissguth
Colleen Sexton
Photo Researcher
Erica Ackerberg
Editorial/Photo Assistant
Marybeth Campbell
Consultants/Contributors
Rex Honey
Sandra K. Davis
Designer
Jim Simondet
Cartographer
Carol F. Barrett
Indexer
Sylvia Timian
Production Manager
Gary J. Hansen

Independent Picture Service

A farmer uses camels to draw water from a well.

Acknowledgments

Title page photo by Drs. A. A. M. van der Heyden, Naarden, the Netherlands.

Elevation contours adapted from *The Times Atlas of the World*, seventh comprehensive edition (New York: Times Books, 1985).

1 2 3 4 5 6 – I/JR – 98 97 96 95 94 93

Two women take a break from their farm work in the Tihama, a flat, dry region on Yemen's western coast. Farmers make the Tihama fertile through irrigation.

Contents

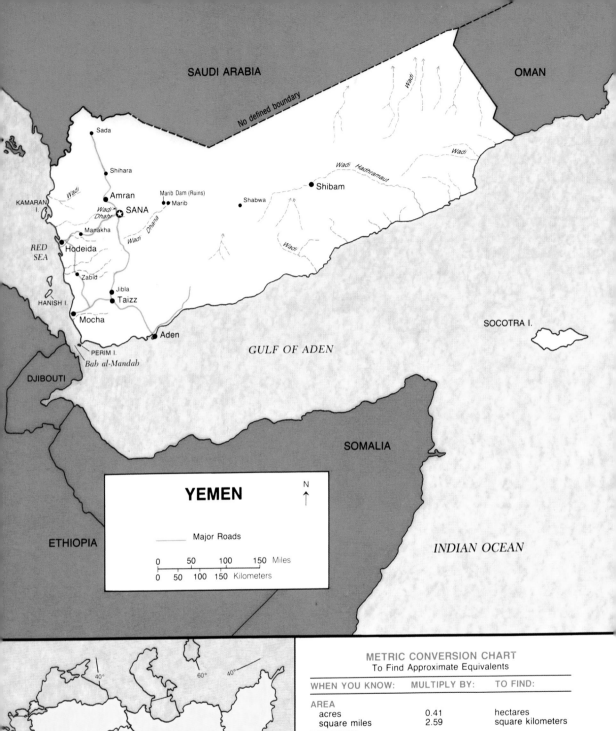

SAUDI ARABIA

OMAN

No defined boundary

Wadi

Wadi

• Sada

• Shihara

Wadi Hadhramaut

Wadi

• Amran

Marib Dam (Ruins)

• Shibam

• Marib

KAMARAN I.

• Shabwa

Wadi Dhahr

☆ SANA

RED SEA

• Manakha

Wadi Dhana

Wadi

• Hodeida

HANISH I.

• Zabid

• Jibla

• Taizz

• Mocha

• Aden

PERIM I.

Bab al-Mandab

GULF OF ADEN

SOCOTRA I.

DJIBOUTI

SOMALIA

YEMEN

N ↑

Major Roads

| 0 | 50 | 100 | 150 | Miles |

| 0 | 50 | 100 | 150 | Kilometers |

ETHIOPIA

INDIAN OCEAN

40° 60° 40°

20°

20°

20°

MIDDLE EAST
YEMEN

| 0 | 500 Miles |

| 0 | 500 Kilometers |

40° INDIAN OCEAN 60°

METRIC CONVERSION CHART
To Find Approximate Equivalents

WHEN YOU KNOW:	MULTIPLY BY:	TO FIND:
AREA		
acres	0.41	hectares
square miles	2.59	square kilometers
CAPACITY		
gallons	3.79	liters
LENGTH		
feet	30.48	centimeters
yards	0.91	meters
miles	1.61	kilometers
MASS (weight)		
pounds	0.45	kilograms
tons	0.91	metric tons
VOLUME		
cubic yards	0.77	cubic meters
TEMPERATURE		
degrees Fahrenheit	0.56 (*after* subtracting 32)	degrees Celsius

A fishing crew cleans and repairs its boat. Yemen's fertile coastal waters support a busy fishing industry.

Introduction

Yemen is a Middle Eastern nation of 10.4 million people. Lying at the southern tip of the Arabian Peninsula, Yemen was once separated into the Yemen Arab Republic (YAR) and the People's Democratic Republic of Yemen (PDRY). In 1990 these two countries united to form the Republic of Yemen.

Cut off from the northern Arabian Peninsula by vast deserts, Yemen has been an isolated, agricultural society for most of its history. Until the 1960s, many areas of the country had few schools, no transportation networks, and little industry. One of the poorest nations in the world, modern Yemen is struggling to

7

The imposing minaret (tower) of an Islamic mosque overlooks the houses and businesses of Sana, Yemen's capital. Islam, the country's major religion, was founded by the Arab prophet Muhammad in the seventh century A.D.

Photo by Bernice K. Condit

build a stable government and a strong economy.

The ancient Sabeans, who lived in Yemen about 1000 B.C., farmed on a large scale. They built dams and canals that routed water from the central mountains to crops at lower elevations. Sabean families formed closely knit clans that fiercely protected their land from neighboring groups.

Beginning in A.D. 300, Yemen's clans and kingdoms battled foreign invaders from

A farmer near Sana harvests grain with a reaphook—a tool with a small, curved blade. Although modern machinery has been introduced in Yemen, many farmers still use traditional methods to plant and harvest their crops.

Ethiopia, Egypt, and Turkey. These wars continued off and on for the next 1,300 years. During these conflicts, clan leaders accepted the Islamic religion and introduced it to Yemenis. By 1517 the Turks, who also followed Islam, had control of the region. After winning independence in the mid-1900s, Yemen was split into the YAR and the PDRY.

Motivated by the discovery of oil along their mutual border, the two Yemens be-gan moving toward unification in 1988. A constitution in 1990 established the Republic of Yemen. The new nation depends on profits from oil to expand agriculture, to educate the population, and to broaden the economy. Yet the people are holding fast to their religious and cultural traditions. Yemenis face the challenge of adapting to new economic opportunities while preserving a very ancient culture.

During the 1960s, demonstrators rode through the streets of South Yemen to protest British rule. The British occupied South Yemen from 1839 until 1967, when an uprising forced them to withdraw.

9

A small village sits among the rough peaks of the Western Highlands. Residents take advantage of the region's heavy rainfall and moderate temperatures to cultivate crops on mountain terraces.

Photo by Lynn Abercrombie

1) The Land

Yemen is a country of mountains, plains, and deserts in southwestern Asia. The nation shares a northeastern land boundary with Oman and an undefined frontier with Saudi Arabia to the north. The waters of the Gulf of Aden—part of the Indian Ocean—meet Yemen's southern coast, and the Red Sea lies to the west. These two bodies of water are joined by the strait of Bab al-Mandab, which separates Yemen from the African continent. Across this narrow strait are the African countries of Djibouti, Ethiopia, and Somalia.

Because Yemen's border with Saudi Arabia is uncertain, officials must estimate the country's size. The Yemeni government claims about 207,000 square miles, an area that makes the country slightly smaller than the state of Texas. The nation's territory also includes the Hanish Islands and the islands of Kamaran and Perim in the Red Sea and the island of Socotra in the Indian Ocean.

Topography

Yemen can be divided into western and eastern regions. In the west, flat plains ex- tend inland from the western and southern coasts. Fertile highlands surrounded by mountains also lie in western Yemen. The eastern half of Yemen is made up of a hilly plateau in the south and a desert in the north. Some mountains in Yemen are volcanically active, and earthquakes have occurred throughout the country.

WESTERN YEMEN

The Tihama, a flat coastal area, ex- tends from the southern tip of Yemen

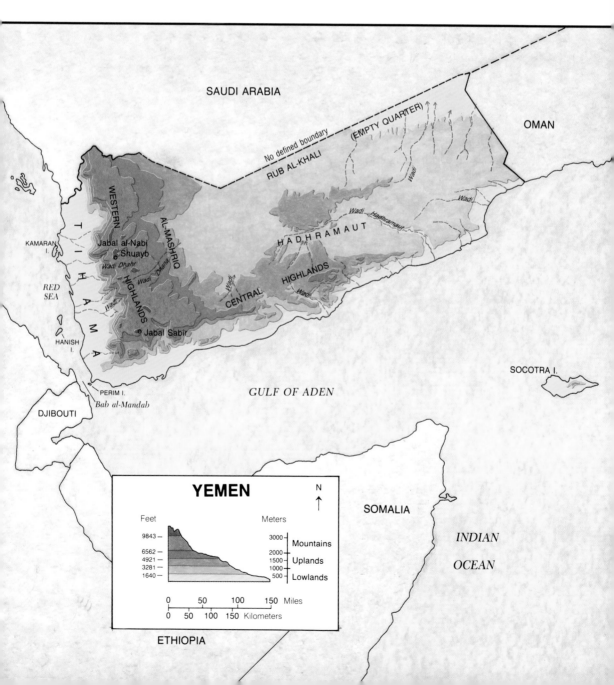

The dry coastal plain of the Tihama ends abruptly at a ridge of low cliffs, which mark the limit of the Western Highlands. Hot winds often blow across the Tihama, bringing fine sand inland from the seashore.

northward into Saudi Arabia. Varying between 15 and 40 miles in width, this sandy plain is made fertile in some areas by irrigation. The plain ends abruptly at a series of rocky cliffs. Over time, precipitation has eroded these cliffs and formed deep wadis—dry riverbeds that fill with seasonal rains.

The cliffs rise sharply to meet the steep mountains of the Western Highlands. This range stretches north to south through the western region. Many of its peaks reach more than 12,000 feet above sea level. At a height of 12,408 feet, Jabal al-Nabi Shuayb is the highest point in Yemen, as well as on the Arabian Peninsula. Farther east, the Western Highlands level off at the fertile, high plateau called the Central Highlands. Watered by wadis and underground springs, this plateau contains Yemen's most productive farmland.

Al-Mashriq, a smaller mountain range, borders the Central Highlands to the east. In the northeastern corner of the west-

Built in the early 1600s, the Bridge of Shihara in the Western Highlands connects the two parts of Shihara, a village built on neighboring peaks.

ern region, rocky al-Mashriq gradually reaches the stone and sand of the Rub al-Khali, or Empty Quarter, of the Arabian Desert.

EASTERN YEMEN

The eastern half of Yemen varies from south to north. A sandy coastal plain along the Gulf of Aden borders a dry, hilly plateau further inland. Deep valleys and narrow wadis, which irrigate the land for farming, cut through the plateau. The largest wadi—the Wadi Hadhramaut—stretches west to east across the entire region before turning southward to empty into the Indian Ocean. The northern half of the eastern region is dominated by the Arabian Desert.

Photo by Bernice K. Condit

A productive agricultural area, the valley of Wadi Dhahr in the Central Highlands is famous for its orchards.

The southernmost region of the vast Arabian Desert—known as the Rub al-Khali—extends into northeastern Yemen. About 1 percent of the Yemeni population lives in this arid land.

Farm workers in Shibam—a village in the Hadhramaut valley—trudge through a cloud of blowing sand. Seasonal floodwaters make the region fertile enough to grow crops.

Climate

Yemen's climate varies with topography and elevation. Rainfall is scarce on the Tihama and on the southern coast, both of which are hot and humid throughout the year. Heavy downpours sometimes occur in areas near the coast and result in brief floods. During the summer months (May to September), temperatures in this area can rise to 120° F during the day and can drop to 80° F at night. In the winter (November to February), coastal temperatures rarely fall below 65° F.

From May to September, moist winds—called monsoons—often blow against the mountains of the Western Highlands, making air masses rise and cool. The cooling air causes torrential rains, most of which fall in the mountain foothills. In some years, however, the summer

Rich soil, moderate rainfall, and a mild climate create lush, green fields in the Central Highlands.

15

monsoons do not arrive at all, creating droughts in the lower elevations.

In the Central Highlands, the weather is dry and mild, with temperatures averaging about 70° F throughout the year. Rainy seasons in April and August fill the wadis with enough water to support a variety of crops. In the winter, winds blow westward from central Asia, bringing cool, dry air. January temperatures can drop below freezing at night, causing damaging frosts.

The summer monsoons do not reach the al-Mashriq or the Rub al-Khali. As a result, rain seldom falls in these areas. Brief, heavy showers that occur in the eastern plateau fill the wadis and enable Yemenis in this area to grow crops. Although the Rub al-Khali may not receive rain for years, strong winter winds are common and sometimes cause sandstorms.

Flora and Fauna

Yemen's varied terrain supports many kinds of plants and animals. Sparse shrubs and hardy grasses grow in coastal areas. Cactuses, tamarisks, and other flowering plants that can survive dry conditions also flourish in this region. Palms and small scrub trees cling to the rocky cliffs east of the Tihama.

The fertile valleys of the Western Highlands receive enough rain to nourish many tropical plants, such as acacias and ficus. Fruit-bearing trees—including dates, mangoes, bananas, and papayas—thrive in the area's rich soil. Farmers have cleared much of this land to plant a shrub called *qat*. Yemenis chew the qat leaves, which contain a mild stimulant.

Several different kinds of trees—including almonds, walnuts, peaches, apricots, pears, lemons, and pomegranates—grow in the Central Highlands. Spice plants and

Photo by Christine Osborne/Middle East Pictures

Some areas of the hot, humid Tihama support stands of palm trees. This oasis (fertile area) of palms lies near the port of Mocha on the southwestern coast.

A caravan of camels passes through southeastern Yemen's dry plains. This region supports only hardy grasses and shrubs.

Photo by Lynn Abercrombie

Sea gulls comb the shore for food near Hodeida, a port on the Red Sea coast.

Photo by Christine Osborne/Middle East Pictures

grapevines also exist in this region. The wadis of the eastern plateau support date trees. Only sparse shrubs and grasses survive in the Arabian Desert.

Wooded areas once covered Yemen's Western and Central highlands. During the last century, farmers cut down most of the trees for fuel and building materials. Only a few stands of trees remain, and the government cannot afford extensive reforestation efforts.

The clearing of woodlands and other natural habitats has reduced Yemen's animal population. Small mammals—such as hares, foxes, and hyenas—still live throughout central Yemen. Hedgehogs, porcupines, hyraxes (a type of shrew), and mongooses are more rare. Arabian gazelles and honey badgers inhabit the Tihama.

Gelada baboons, which travel in groups, make their homes in the mountains and highlands of the northwest.

About 300 types of birds thrive in Yemen, and 12 are unique to the country. Many other species migrate between Europe to the northwest and Africa to the west and south. The birds stop in Yemen to rest and to find food before continuing their journey. Flamingos and sea gulls dwell in coastal areas, and ravens and vultures live in the highlands. Weaver birds build their elaborate nests in trees and on telephone poles in eastern Yemen.

Natural Resources

Oil, which geologists recently discovered in west central Yemen, is the country's most valuable natural resource. The nation has dug several wells and has built a pipeline to transport crude oil to Hodeida, a port on the Red Sea. Yemen also has large reserves of natural gas, and development of this important energy source is under way.

Limestone, clay, kaolin (white clay), sand, and marble exist in great quantities throughout Yemen. These resources provide building and industrial materials. In addition, workers mine large supplies of rock salt on the western coast. Yemen has small deposits of coal, copper, cobalt, iron

Near the ancient city of Marib in central Yemen, a well draws oil from beneath the Arabian Desert. Petroleum is the country's most important natural resource.

Streets inside Sana's medina (old walled section) bustle with activity. The city's growing population has caused many residents to abandon the medina for Sana's suburbs.

ore, gold, nickel, and zinc, but these minerals are too scarce to be mined economically.

Cities

Although many of Yemen's 10.4 million people still live in small villages, the nation's cities are growing rapidly. Yemenis are moving to urban areas to find work in newly developed industries. In the early 1990s, more than 25 percent of Yemenis resided in cities, the largest of which are Sana and Aden.

SANA

Sana, the capital of Yemen, lies 140 miles from the coast of the Red Sea in a fertile area of the Central Highlands. Since the early 1970s, when about 55,000 people lived in the city, Sana has experienced a population explosion. Many Yemenis look-

ing for work moved from rural areas to the capital. As a result, Sana's population had reached nearly 500,000 by the early 1990s. The city has spread in all directions, absorbing nearby villages and farmland.

Despite its rapid growth, Sana has preserved its medina—or old walled section—that was established in the first century A.D. Many of the city's houses are more than 400 years old. Standing six to seven stories high, these dwellings are constructed of stone, brick, and mud and are ornately decorated with white plaster. Builders traditionally made windowpanes out of small squares of colored alabaster, a soft stone. Modern city dwellers use colored glass to copy the traditional style.

The central market, known as Suq al-Milh, dominates the southeastern section of the medina and contains more than 40 small markets. Each craft or trade occupies a particular area—sometimes even a

19

Famous for its unique architecture, Sana's medina contains dwellings that are more than 400 years old. Many of the houses, which are ornately decorated with white plaster, stand seven stories high.

Shoppers examine a vendor's goods in the Suq al-Milh—Sana's enormous marketplace.

particular street—within the suq. Small rooms above the merchants' stalls house students, as well as the sick and the elderly. Within the stalls, vendors sell a wide variety of goods, including pottery, clothes, carpets, and silver and copper items. Farmers in the suq offer vegetables, spices, qat, and raisins for sale.

The elaborate minarets (towers) of mosques (Islamic houses of prayer) rise above the markets and houses of Sana. The massive outer walls of the largest mosque, al-Jami al-Kabir, enclose fountains and buildings.

Many residents of Sana use public baths, which are located throughout the old city. The baths usually feature a large central room with fountains and a wide, cold-water pool. Smaller heated chambers are located underground. To let in light the baths are roofed with domes made from baked brick and glass. An elaborate system of pipes carries water from nearby wells to both the hot and cold rooms.

The baths are open 18 hours a day, and city dwellers often meet there for coffee or tea.

The growth of Sana has caused some wealthy residents of the medina to move to the city's outskirts, where recreation, shopping, and entertainment facilities are readily available. The old dwellings in the capital have been divided for renters but are poorly maintained, and many homes have sustained water damage from leaky pipes. To preserve Sana's unique architecture, the United Nations (UN) has funded restoration and preservation of the old walled city.

ADEN

Located in the crater of an extinct volcano on the southern coast, Aden (population 400,000) is Yemen's chief seaport and economic center. Aden became a key trading hub during ancient times and continues to be important to commerce and transportation in the Middle East. Foreign ships stop at the port to refuel and to load fish products, coffee, tobacco, cotton, and salt. Domestic and international flights land at the city's large airport. Modern roads lead from Aden to other cities and to villages throughout the country. Aden is also a manufacturing

Yemen's chief seaport, Aden is nestled within the crater of an extinct volcano. Huge lava mountains, created long ago by a volcanic eruption, shelter a natural harbor that is deep enough for oceangoing vessels.

Photo by Lynn Abercrombie

Perched in the foothills of Jabal Sabir, one of southwestern Yemen's tallest mountains, Taizz is a city of concrete buildings and modern industries.

center, where huge refineries process petroleum and where factories produce cooking oil and textiles.

Aden's architecture reflects both its history and status as a modern urban settlement. Large, up-to-date structures line wide thoroughfares, while old buildings stand along winding, narrow streets.

The city's population includes Arabs, Asians, Africans, and Europeans.

Secondary Cities

Taizz, Yemen's third largest city, lies in southwestern Yemen and is home to more than 300,000 people. Compared with Sana or Aden, Taizz is young, dating to the seventh century, when it was a religious and administrative center. Periodically, Taizz has served as the nation's capital, most recently from 1948 to 1962. Famous for its mosques and markets, Taizz also has extensive modern neighborhoods.

Hodeida (population 300,000) is a commercial port on the Red Sea. Most of the city's buildings were constructed during the twentieth century and are made of concrete. A marketplace stands in the oldest area of Hodeida, which also contains beautiful houses with wooden balconies and plaster-decorated walls. Fishing remains an important industry in the city. Each morning, fishing fleets deliver catches of shark, red snapper, and kingfish to the local market.

Located in west central Yemen, Marib symbolizes the country's past and present history. In ancient times, Marib was the capital of the kingdom of Saba. In about 500 B.C., the Sabeans dammed an important wadi. Considered the most valuable archaeological site in Yemen, the ruins of the Marib Dam now draw tourists. Marib is also a modern city of governmental offices, small shops, and comfortable houses.

Photo by Lynn Abercrombie

Traditional wooden boats dock in Hodeida, an important fishing center on the western coast.

Independent Picture Service

Modern Marib, a city in west central Yemen, rises above the ruins of ancient Marib, which was inhabited by the Sabeans as early as 1000 B.C.

Photo by Lynn Abercrombie

Crumbling sluice gates, which once controlled the flow of water through the ancient Marib Dam, stand on the banks of the Wadi Dhana in central Yemen. Built by the Sabeans in about 500 B.C., the dam was constructed of carefully cut stone bricks, some of which still carry ancient writing.

2) History and Government

Separated from the rest of the Arabian Peninsula by vast deserts, Yemen was far from the large empires that rose and fell in the Middle East and North Africa. Early Yemeni merchants traded with these empires along both land and sea routes. Most ancient Yemenis, however, were farmers who grew crops for their families and clans.

Yemen's past, like that of much of the Arabian Peninsula, is tied to the religion of Islam. Yemenis consider the establishment of this faith in the seventh century A.D. to be the most important event in their history.

Ancient Kingdoms

Archaeologists believe humans have inhabited Yemen for hundreds of thousands of years. By about 5000 B.C., people in the region were using flint tools and building water channels and stone dwellings. In about 1000 B.C., three kingdoms arose. Saba (also called Sheba) and Qataban developed in the Central Highlands.

Hadhramaut was established in eastern Yemen. Five centuries later, two more realms appeared—Maain in the Central Highlands and Ausan near the tip of the Arabian Peninsula in the Western Highlands.

Each of these southern Arabian kingdoms enjoyed periods of dominance and prosperity. They also shared a common culture, which included polytheism (the worship of many gods). Because the ancient kingdoms did not build walls or fortifications, archaeologists believe that the early Yemenis lived in peace.

Saba, the largest and most powerful kingdom, prospered from trade and farming. An extensive irrigation system enabled the Sabeans to grow abundant crops. The system included dams that diverted runoff from occasional rains into artificial canals. The largest dam was constructed in about 500 B.C. near Marib, the capital of Saba. The dam allowed the ancient Sabeans to water about 25,000 acres of land.

Trading Routes

The early traders of southern Arabia controlled an important network of overland caravan trails. The trade routes started in southern and western Arabia and crossed the Arabian Peninsula to Babylonia and Mesopotamia (both in modern Iraq), Egypt, Palestine (modern Israel), and Syria.

Yemen's early kingdoms grew wealthy from the trade of frankincense and myrrh—strong-smelling resins from trees that grew only in eastern Yemen, southern Oman, and northern Africa. Ancient peoples used these resins to make perfumes, medicines, and the incense that was burned in many religious ceremonies. In addition to these exports, Yemeni traders sold spices, textiles, and swords from India; silks from China; and gold, ivory, and slaves from Africa. Believing that all these valuable goods originated in southern Arabia, merchants from the north called Yemen *Arabia Felix,* meaning "Happy Arabia" in Latin.

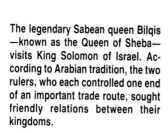

The legendary Sabean queen Bilqis —known as the Queen of Sheba— visits King Solomon of Israel. According to Arabian tradition, the two rulers, who each controlled one end of an important trade route, sought friendly relations between their kingdoms.

Use of the caravan trails declined in the first century A.D., when a Mediterranean sailor named Hippalus discovered a sea route from Egypt to India. Hippalus found that the summer monsoons could blow ships down the Red Sea, around the Arabian Peninsula, and east to India. Winter monsoons could bring ships back along the same course. The newly discovered sea-lanes contributed to the rise of Himyar, a kingdom in the highlands that held land along the strait of Bab al-Mandab. By A.D. 50, the Himyarites had conquered southwestern Arabia and had taken charge of shipping through the strait.

Meanwhile, the Romans (from the Italian Peninsula) had conquered an enormous empire that stretched from northern Europe into North Africa. In A.D. 323, the Roman emperor Constantine proclaimed Christianity to be the official religion of his empire. Because Christianity did not allow the use of incense for certain religious rituals, trade of frankincense and myrrh declined and the kingdoms of southern Arabia lost much of their wealth.

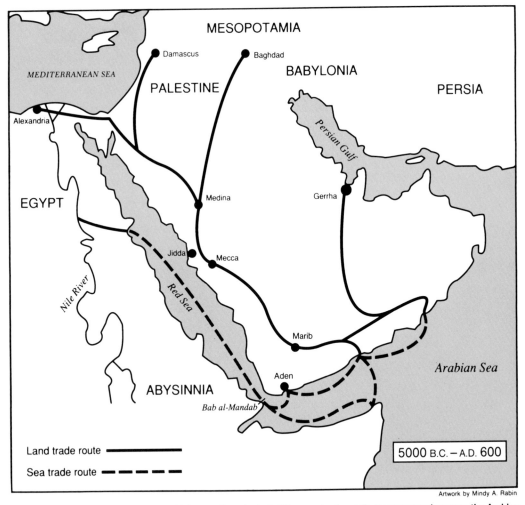

Artwork by Mindy A. Rabin

Early traders formed large caravans, which sometimes included thousands of camels, to carry goods across the Arabian Peninsula. When a sea route was discovered through the Strait of Bab al-Mandab, Aden became an important stop for ships sailing to eastern destinations.

Courtesy of Hunt Oil Company/by Lynn Abercrombie

Ancient incense dealers harvested myrrh—a fragrant, brown resin—from scrubby trees of the *Commiphora* family *(above)*. **Paved remains of the ancient incense trail** *(right)* **still exist in Yemen.**

Photo by Lynn Abercrombie

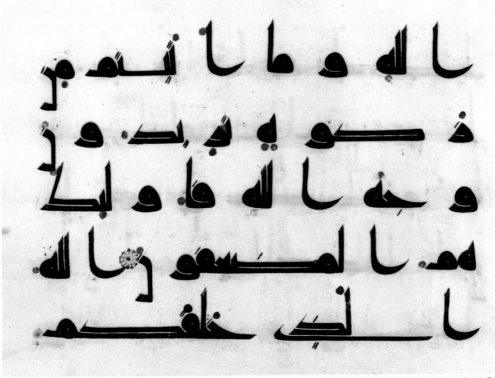

Early Muslims (followers of Islam) copied the Koran—the Islamic sacred book—in a flowing Arabic script. The religion spread to Yemen soon after its founding in the seventh century A.D.

Early Conquerors

The Himyarites continued to rule Yemen and allowed missionaries of differing faiths to enter the kingdom. In the fourth and fifth centuries, Christian and Jewish missionaries arrived and were successful in converting the inhabitants of southern Arabia to the Jewish and Christian religions. Many Himyarite kings also accepted these monotheistic (one-god) faiths.

In the early 500s, the Sabean king Yusuf Ashaar Dhu Nuwas ordered all Christians in his realm to convert to Judaism (the Jewish religion). More than 20,000 Christians refused and were executed. In response, the Christian king of Ethiopia, Abraha of Axum, seized Yemen in 525. Under Abraha, workers tried to repair the Marib Dam, which had begun to fall apart. Despite these efforts, floods in 570 destroyed the dam, forcing many Yemeni farmers to leave southern Arabia.

In the same year, Abraha and his army mounted elephants to attack the kingdoms of northern Arabia. Abraha's attempt to conquer this region failed, and the king died soon afterward. After Abraha's death, the Himyarites asked the emperor of Persia (modern Iran) to help them oust the Ethiopians. In 575 the Persians defeated the Ethiopians and brought the Yemeni kingdoms under Persian rule.

The Spread of Islam

In 628 the Persian governor of Yemen accepted the religion of Islam, which the Arab prophet Muhammad had founded in Mecca, Saudi Arabia. The new faith spread quickly, as many Yemeni sheikhs (local leaders) converted and introduced the religion to their people. Muhammad's missionaries arrived in Yemen, and by the early 630s workers had built the first Yemeni mosques in Sana.

After the death of Muhammad in 632, Muslims (followers of Islam) divided into two sects. Sunni Muslims elected their religious leaders, while Shiite Muslims believed that the head of Islam should be chosen from Muhammad's descendants. The Sunnis eventually became the dominant group and named their own caliph (leader) of Islam.

To expand Muslim territory, the first caliph, Abu Bakr, led Islamic warriors in the conquest of Egypt, North Africa, and Spain. The Arabs also attacked Syria, Mesopotamia, and Persia, as well as parts of India and central Asia. More than 20,000 Yemeni soldiers joined the Arab armies.

Yemeni Kingdoms

In 661 the Umayyad dynasty (family of rulers) took over the caliphate and moved their capital from Mecca to Damascus (in present-day Syria). Islam's religious center remained in Mecca, and Yemen became a province of the Umayyad Empire. When the Abbasid clan seized power from the Umayyads in 715, they established their capital in Baghdad (in modern Iraq). Yemen's distance from Islam's political and cultural hubs allowed several small, nearly independent kingdoms to develop in southern Arabia.

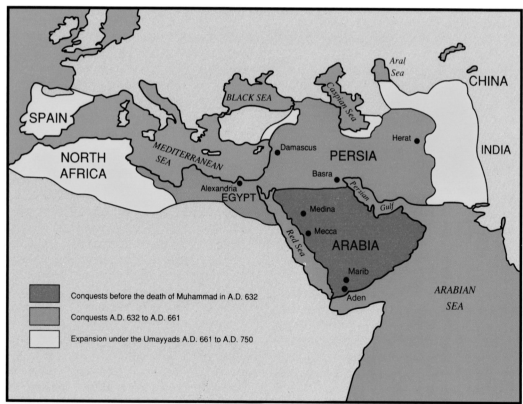

Conquests before the death of Muhammad in A.D. 632

Conquests A.D. 632 to A.D. 661

Expansion under the Umayyads A.D. 661 to A.D. 750

Artwork by Mindy A. Rabin

Muslim armies, which included thousands of Yemeni soldiers, joined under the caliph (leader of Islam) in the seventh and eighth centuries. The Muslims conquered territories to the north, east, and west of Arabia.

THE ZIYADIDS

Dissatisfied with Abbasid rule, two groups in the Tihama region rebelled against the Abbasid governor in Yemen in 819. The caliph in Baghdad sent Muhammad ibn Ziyad to restore order. After putting down the revolt, ibn Ziyad founded the town of Zabid. Under his rule, Zabid became an independent realm that lasted for several hundred years.

Ibn Ziyad used the important al-Ashair Mosque in Zabid as a university, where scholars studied the Sunni branch of Islam. The school also taught mathematics, grammar, history, poetry, and Islamic law.

THE ZAYDIS

In 892 the caliph sent a descendant of Muhammad, Yahya al-Rassi, to mediate a war between two rival clans in northwestern Yemen. Al-Rassi became the first imam (spiritual leader) of the Zaydi dynasty, which lasted longer than any other Yemeni ruling clan.

The Zaydis held beliefs similar to those of the Sunni Muslims. The Zaydis, however, recognized only four previous imams —all descendants of Zayd ibn Ali, whose followers founded Zaydism. Zaydi rule was organized around many different clans. The loyalty of each clan to the imam was more sacred than bonds with other Islamic believers. The study of war was also very important and enabled the Zaydis to survive centuries of attacks and to rise to power again and again.

THE SULAYHIDS

In 1046 the Sulayhid state was founded in Sana by Ali al-Sulayhi, a follower of the Ismaili faith—a branch of Shiite Islam. For the next 17 years, the Sulayhids fought with other sects that did not accept Ismaili beliefs. Al-Sulayhi's army conquered his opponents and united the Yemeni kingdoms under his rule in 1063.

In 1067 Queen Arwa, the wife of Ali's son and successor, inherited the throne after her husband died. A popular queen, she decreased the use of the military and attempted to establish clan loyalty through fair administration. Her efforts were not successful, and Sulayhid rule slowly disintegrated until Arwa's death in 1138. With no heirs to the throne, the Sulayhid dynasty ended.

THE AYYUBIDS AND THE RASULIDS

In 1173 the Ayyubid rulers from Egypt conquered Yemen and made it a self-governing state within the Ayyubid Empire. Unable to rule a remote area like Yemen effectively, the Ayyubids left control in the hands of a local official named Nur al-Din Umar ibn al-Rasul, who proclaimed Yemen an independent nation. Centered in Taizz, the Rasulid family ruled from 1228 to 1454.

Foreign Invasions

By the early 1500s, Europeans—including Portuguese merchants—were using the sea route between Egypt and India for trade and conquest. In 1507 the Portuguese annexed (took over) the island of Socotra in the Indian Ocean. From Socotra, they tried to seize Yemen. In 1513 the Portuguese adventurer Afonso de Albuquerque led an unsuccessful invasion of Aden. Egypt, to protect its interests in the Red Sea, sent a large fleet to Yemen and captured the Tihama and the highlands around Sana. Egypt's attack on Aden, however, failed.

In 1517 armies of the Ottoman Empire (centered in what is now Turkey) conquered Egypt, and by 1548 the Ottoman Turks had brought most of Yemen under their control. Under Ottoman rule, which lasted for more than a century, Yemenis harvested coffee beans from the highlands and developed an extensive coffee trade. Mocha, a port on the Red Sea, became the most important coffee port in the world. The superior coffee exported from this city became known as mocha coffee.

During her reign from A.D. 1067 to A.D. 1138, Queen Arwa moved the capital of the Sulayhid state from Sana to Jibla in southwestern Yemen. At Jibla she encouraged the development of terrace farming on nearby mountains and commemorated her reign by building a great mosque.

In 1590 Qasim the Great, a young descendant of the Zaydi imams, began a resistance movement against the Ottomans. For the first time, Shiites and Sunnis were united, and Qasim attracted Yemenis from throughout the region to his cause. Qasim was elected imam and by 1608 had gathered enough support to force the Turks into a 10-year truce. According to the terms of the agreement, Qasim controlled his provinces, and the Ottomans handled foreign affairs. Turkish occupation ended in 1636, when Yemen was united under the leadership of Qasim's son Muayyad Muhammad.

Under the Zaydis, centralized control of Yemen fell apart as some groups proclaimed their independence. Zaydi rule was also threatened by the British, who wanted to establish a commercial port in southern Arabia to supply their colony in India. In 1799 the British seized the island of Perim near the Bab al-Mandab, and in 1839 they conquered Aden.

Courtesy of Cultural and Tourism Office of the Turkish Embassy

During the mid-1500s, the Ottoman navy conquered the southern and western coasts of Yemen. Under the leadership of Suleyman the Magnificent, the Ottomans destroyed Aden and marched inland to capture Sana.

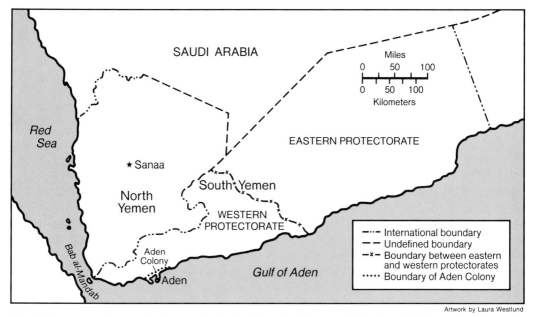

The British seized Aden from the Ottoman Turks in 1839 and quickly extended their control into eastern Yemen. By the early 1900s, the British had created the Aden Colony and the Eastern and Western protectorates.

In 1849 the Ottoman Turks returned to Yemen and occupied the Tihama. By 1882 the Turks had taken control of much of northwestern Yemen, including Sada, the Zaydi capital. The Turks failed to extend their power into the Hadhramaut (eastern Yemen) during the 1870s.

The Turkish drive southward alarmed the British, who controlled much of southern Yemen. To protect their trade routes, the British signed treaties with many Yemeni sheikhs. The leaders agreed that they would not sell or give away any territory without British approval. They would also notify British officials if any foreigners attempted to interfere with the sheikhs' affairs. In exchange, the British promised military protection.

Between 1901 and 1905, the Turks and the British drew the border between their two territories, which came to be called respectively North Yemen and South Yemen. The boundary, which was recognized both locally and internationally, remained intact for most of the twentieth century.

North Yemen's occupation by the Turks did not go unchallenged, however. Throughout the early 1900s, the Zaydis—along with several northern Tihama groups under the leadership of Sayyid Muhammad al-Idrisi—staged many uprisings. In 1911, to end the fighting, the Zaydis and the Turks signed the Treaty of Daan, which gave the Zaydis rule over northern Yemen.

Two Yemens

The Ottoman Empire collapsed after its defeat in World War I (1914–1918), which pitted the Turks and Germany against Britain, France, and Russia. North Yemen remained under the rule of the Zaydi king Yahya, and South Yemen remained under British control.

SOUTH YEMEN

The British divided South Yemen into three parts—a colony and two protectorates (regions dependent on a foreign government). The Aden Colony surrounded and included the port city of Aden. The Western Protectorate contained the southern third of the Central Highlands and al-Mashriq. It stretched from the tip of the Arabian Peninsula east to the Wadi Hadhramaut. The Eastern Protectorate included all of present-day eastern Yemen.

Britain ruled the protectorates through local leaders and intervened only in cases of internal power struggles and border disputes with North Yemen. In the Aden Colony, Yemenis eager for self-government expressed discontent with British control through frequent strikes. Despite the unrest, Aden and some parts of the protectorates experienced growth and modernization.

NORTH YEMEN

The British also showed interest in expanding their territory to include North Yemen. Attempts to negotiate for land

Photo by UPI/Bettmann

North Yemeni forces prepare for battle as Saudi Arabia and North Yemen dispute a portion of the Tihama. The conflict resulted in the Saudi-Yemeni war of 1934 and ended with the Taif Treaty, which set a short, northwestern boundary between the two nations.

with King Yahya were refused. As a result, the British allowed opponents of the Zaydis to use Aden as a base. In 1948 a member of one of these opposition groups assassinated the king.

Yahya had secured his power in North Yemen by isolating his people from outside influences. Yahya's son Ahmad changed his father's policy by accepting foreign aid and by allowing foreign countries to prospect for oil. He also formed diplomatic ties with Britain, the United States, and the Soviet Union.

Despite Ahmad's efforts to open North Yemen to the rest of the world, the kingdom itself made little progress. By the end of Ahmad's reign in 1962, North Yemen still had poor roads, no schools, few doctors, and no manufacturing facilities.

The Yemen Arab Republic (YAR)

King Ahmad's death brought his son Muhammad al-Badr to power. One week into King Muhammad's reign, a group of army officers led by Colonel Abdullah al-Sallal staged a revolution and quickly overthrew the Zaydi monarchy. The new regime founded the Yemen Arab Republic (YAR), with al-Sallal as prime minister. With the exception of the kingdoms of Saudi Arabia and Jordan, which had supported the monarchy, Arab countries welcomed the new nation. After al-Sallal's revolt, the YAR became a member of the UN.

King Muhammad fled to the northern mountains, where his uncle was organizing a royalist force backed by Britain and Saudi Arabia. Civil war broke out in 1962, when the Royalists clashed with al-Sallal's Republican army. The Republicans were supported by Egypt and the Soviet Union, nations that wanted to ally themselves with the YAR. Fierce fighting caused many casualties on both sides.

By 1967 the war had reached a stalemate, and disputes were occurring among various groups within the Republican ranks. Al-Sallal and his backers believed that the YAR would survive only if it established friendly relations with Saudi Arabia, an oil-rich kingdom that covered most of the Arabian Peninsula. This view was unpopular among many Republicans because Saudi Arabia was helping the Royalists. In late 1967, these anti-Saudi factions replaced al-Sallal with Abd al-Rahman al-Iryani.

With support from the Soviet Union and from dissatisfied groups opposed to British rule in South Yemen, al-Iryani's new government was able to hold back the Royalists. Internal feuding further weakened the Royalists, while peace initiatives between the Saudis and the Republicans ended Saudi support for the Royalist cause. In 1970, after more than 200,000 North Yemenis had been killed, the war ended, and King Muhammad was exiled to Iraq. In July 1970, Saudi Arabia formed diplomatic ties with the YAR.

Photo by UPI/Bettmann

Colonel Abdullah al-Sallal overthrew the Zaydi monarchy and became prime minister of the newly founded Yemen Arab Republic (YAR) in 1962.

Courtesy of Hunt Oil Company/by Lynn Abercrombie

In Sana, a monument to the revolution that established the YAR displays war equipment, as well as text and photographs that describe the events of the uprising.

The People's Democratic Republic of Yemen (PDRY)

In South Yemen, violence also erupted during the 1960s. The British had established the Federation of South Arabia to unite the protectorates with the Aden Colony. But this action was opposed by residents of Aden who wanted independence for the colony. Britain's promise that it would eventually grant independence to the federation did not halt the violence.

A rebel movement quickly developed in Aden, where activists formed the National Liberation Front (NLF). In 1963 the nationalists staged an uprising, and warfare broke out in and near Aden. By 1967 the NLF had forced the British to withdraw from South Yemen, which officially gained its independence in November 1967. The NLF declared the founding of the People's Republic of South Yemen.

The new country, under the leadership of Qahtan al-Shabi, allied itself with the Soviet Union and with other Communist nations. The loss of British trade and investment, however, caused South Yemen to face serious economic problems. Al-Shabi put some sectors of the economy under government control. In addition,

Photo by UPI/Bettmann

Armed with rifles, Aden Federal Guards receive training from the British in 1967. The guards were organized to stop an uprising against the British colonial government in South Yemen.

South Yemen began receiving aid from the Communist countries of eastern Europe.

South Yemen formed even closer ties to the Communist bloc in 1969, when al-Shabi was ousted by Salim Rubay Ali. Strongly pro-Communist, Rubay Ali changed the

Photo by UPI/Bettmann

Rebel armies storm through Aden to fight for independence from British rule. After the British withdrew in 1967, the rebels formed a government and allied themselves with the Soviet Union, a Communist nation.

After the revolution, workers in Sana clear rubble from a ditch and prepare to build a street. The YAR's new government modernized roads and established new industries.

name of the country to the People's Democratic Republic of Yemen (PDRY).

Civil Wars to Unification

By the early 1970s, the two independent Yemeni states had restructured their governments. But both countries faced the enormous task of rebuilding their economies, which had been damaged by the many years of conflict. To accomplish this goal, both nations had to rely on foreign aid. The YAR received most of its money from Saudi Arabia and from European countries, while the PDRY obtained funds from the Soviet Union. Because the Saudis and the Soviets were hostile to one another, the two Yemens were also at odds.

This conflict led to border disputes between the YAR and the PDRY in the early 1970s. Negotiations stopped the fighting in October 1972, when the two Yemens agreed to merge within a year. The merger was postponed because the prime ministers of both countries were unable to persuade their political leaders to accept unification. Border skirmishes resumed, and relations declined between the two countries.

The YAR changed leadership many times during the remainder of the 1970s. In 1974 al-Iryani was ousted by a member of his cabinet who disagreed with the leader's policies. Two of al-Iryani's successors were murdered by unknown assassins. The YAR accused the PDRY of plotting the second assassination. As a result, the two Yemens clashed briefly. After the fighting ended, leaders of the two nations signed another unification agreement.

During the 1980s, the YAR, under the leadership of Ali Abdullah Saleh, steadily improved its economy and its relations with other countries. The PDRY, on the other hand, was plagued by internal political turmoil and economic decline. In 1986 a civil war between two competing political factions in Aden killed at least 3,000 people. Economic decline in the Soviet Union caused the Soviets to close their naval base at Aden and to reduce financial aid to the PDRY.

A newly built pipeline carries oil from the northern desert to the Red Sea coast. The discovery of oil in the early 1980s prompted the YAR and the People's Democratic Republic of Yemen (PDRY) to merge, a process that was completed in 1990.

The troubled economies in both countries moved the two Yemens closer to unification in the mid-1980s. Their motive was oil, which had been found in the northern desert bordering both nations. Instead of dividing the oil fields, the governments declared the area to be neutral ground.

In November 1989, Yemeni leaders agreed on a timetable for merging the two countries. Their plan, however, was opposed by religious authorities, local leaders in the YAR, and strict Communist officials in the PDRY. Fearing that this opposition would eventually disrupt the unification process, the legislatures of both countries quickly approved a new constitution on May 20, 1990. They named the unified country the Republic of Yemen.

Government officials opened the borders and made the two currencies legal in both countries. They declared Sana the political capital and Aden the economic capital. In May 1991, a large majority of the citizens of Yemen voted to support the merger.

Recent Events

Under the leadership of former YAR president Saleh, Yemen slowly began to expand its economy with financial aid from foreign countries. Yemen depended on trade and aid from Iraq, as well as from Saudi Arabia and Kuwait. Some of this aid was jeopardized in 1990 when Iraq invaded Kuwait, a small, oil-rich Middle Eastern country. This invasion led to the Persian Gulf War between Iraq and UN-backed forces based in Saudi Arabia.

Although Yemen was against the Iraqi invasion of Kuwait, the Yemeni government also sharply criticized the presence of foreign troops in Saudi Arabia. In response the Saudis evicted Yemeni workers from Saudi Arabia. More than 700,000

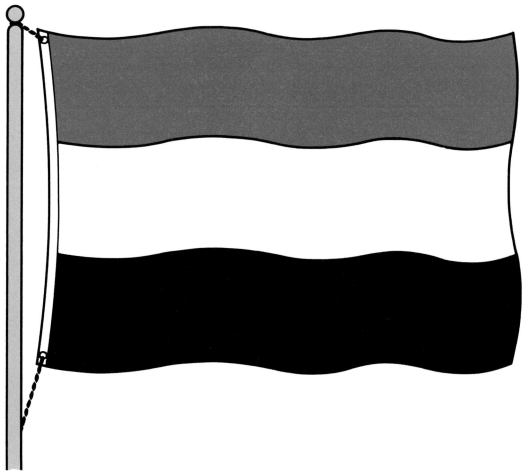

Artwork by Laura Westlund

Adopted upon unification in May 1990, the national flag of Yemen features colors common throughout the Arab world. Red stands for courage, white represents generosity, and black symbolizes historic Islamic conquests.

laborers returned to Yemen, causing severe unemployment and economic hardship. In addition, refugees from the war-torn African nation of Somalia were entering the country, putting a further strain on Yemen's economy.

Tensions between Saudi Arabia and Yemen increased in 1992, when Yemen began to extract oil from a field near the disputed Saudi-Yemeni border. In fact, Saudi Arabia claims 25 percent of the territory that once was South Yemen. In mid-1992, the two countries agreed to begin negotiations over the disputed region.

Government

The 1990 constitution that joined the YAR and the PDRY recognizes Islam as

Photo by Hazel Strouts

Refugees from Somalia, an east African nation suffering from famine and political unrest, entered Yemen in 1992 in search of food and medical aid. Hundreds of Somalis did not survive the journey across the Arabian Sea to Yemen's southern coast.

Crude oil pumped from wells in central Yemen travels by pipeline five miles into the Red Sea before reaching this terminal. The unified Yemeni government hopes that rapid development of the oil industry will boost the country's troubled economy.

Yemen's official religion and Arabic as its official language. Upon unification, the two countries merged their governments and announced a 30-month transition period before the first national elections. During this time, the new government planned to finalize the nation's legal and administrative structure. The first elections were scheduled to be held at the end of 1992. Officials needed more time to organize the combined government, however, and postponed elections until mid-1993.

Yemen's constitution provides for a multiparty democracy ruled by a five-member presidential council. The members of this council are elected to five-year terms by the country's legislature—the 301-member council of representatives. The presi-dential council names a chairperson to represent Yemen outside the country and also chooses a prime minister to lead the government. The prime minister selects a cabinet of advisers and administrators.

The constitution also discusses local governments, but their functions and election procedures have not yet been finalized. During the transition period, a group will study local issues and will draw new internal boundaries.

Yemen's judicial branch is made up of a high council that oversees administrative matters and a supreme court that decides the constitutionality of laws. In addition, the new government has established 270 primary courts and 13 courts of appeal.

A group of boys and their elders gathers in a small village. About half of Yemen's population is under the age of 15.

3) The People

Most Yemenis live on farms and in small villages that are scattered across the country. The population density is low, with only 51 people per square mile. Since the unification of the two Yemens, however, urban industries have grown, and many people are leaving rural areas in search of jobs in the cities. Twenty-five percent of Yemen's 10.4 million people are now city dwellers.

In addition, Yemen's population is growing quickly and is expected to double within 20 years. Most Yemeni families are large, averaging about eight members. Several generations of a family often live together in a single house. Within a community, families elect a sheikh to resolve local disputes. Some sheikhs head large clans that can influence governmental decisions.

Religious and Social Structures

The state religion of Yemen is Islam, and most Yemenis are Muslims. Although the Jewish population is small, it represents the largest non-Muslim group in the country. In the late 1940s, many Jews left Yemen for Israel, which had become an independent Jewish state in 1948. Small Christian and Hindu communities exist in southern Yemen.

Islam means "submission to the will of Allah (God)." Devout Muslims follow the teachings of the Arab prophet Muhammad that are contained in the Koran (the Muslim holy book). Islam includes several pillars (duties of faith). Among them are fasting from sunrise to sunset during the holy month of Ramadan and making a pilgrimage to the holy city of Mecca at least once in a lifetime. Muslims also pray together in mosques, especially on Friday, the Islamic holy day.

Islam has two main branches—Sunni and Shiite—that are distinguished mainly by their manner of choosing leaders. Yemen has three distinct subgroups within the branches, namely the Shafais, the Zaydis, and the Ismailis.

About half of the country's population are Shafais, a Sunni sect that dominates southern Yemen. One-third of Yemeni Muslims are Zaydis, a Shiite subgroup that once ruled the country and still strongly influences the government. One important difference between the Shafais and the Zaydis lies in each sect's view of the Koran. The Shafais believe that the Koran is the word of God as dictated to Muhammad, whereas the Zaydis hold the Koran as a work created by the Prophet. Ismaili Shiites, who have beliefs similar to the Zaydis, make up only about 2 percent of the population. Most Ismailis live near Manakha in the Central Highlands.

Religion plays an important role in Yemen's social structure. As the descendants of Muhammad and members of the Zaydi sect, the elite *sayyids* receive many privileges. For many years they have had access to an advanced education and have held many administrative and legal positions. Some sayyids engage in trade, and

Muslims gather to worship at a brightly lit mosque. The Islamic faith calls on its followers to pray five times daily.

many own large tracts of rich farmland outside the cities. Although the revolutions in the 1960s ended Zaydi rule, the wealthy sayyids still hold important places in Yemeni society.

The *qadhis,* another elite group, fill judgeships and scholarly posts. The ancestors of this group ruled Yemeni kingdoms before the spread of Islam. Qudha are considered educated people who have earned the respect of the community for their wisdom.

Occupations and family connections determine the social status of most other Yemenis. The sheikhs, who belong to the leading families of each clan, form an important group that has the power to settle disputes in the community. Artisans and merchants organize into guilds (trade groups) that are ranked according to the nature of their craft. For example, the *manasib* are skilled craftspeople. Manasibs are often goldsmiths and blacksmiths. The *muzayyin,* on the other hand, hold less-skilled jobs, such as barbering, butchering, and bricklaying. The *akhdam,* who were traditionally street cleaners, are manual laborers.

Photo by Bernice K. Condit

This stonecutter in Sana probably belongs to the *manasib,* a Yemeni social group that includes skilled craftspeople.

Students at the University of Sana study outdoors. Long discouraged from seeking an education, many Yemeni women are now taking advantage of new open-enrollment policies and training programs.

In recent years, the country's social structure has begun to change. As new economic opportunities have become available, money and material goods have become more important. As a result, high-paying jobs that were once considered low in status are commanding new respect.

Status of Women

The unification of Yemen has created new educational opportunities for the nation's women. In recent years, more Yemeni women have begun to receive schooling and to fill positions in business and educa-tion. Traditional Islamic values still dominate some aspects of daily life. The literacy rate, especially in the cities, is rising fast as more girls attend schools. In rural areas only 1 girl attends school for every 10 boys. Universities now accept women students, but men are still given priority in admission.

In urban centers, an increasing number of Yemeni women work outside their homes. Women are still separated from men, especially during social activities. Most Yemeni women do not eat in public restaurants and usually cover themselves with capes and veils, leaving only their

45

As part of many traditional celebrations—especially weddings—women often use dye to paint designs on their hands and faces *(left)*. Dressed in veils and black, full-length capes, women draw water from a public well *(below)*.

A bundle of *qat* at his side, a man relaxes by smoking a water pipe. Some Yemeni men gather daily to chew qat and smoke, leaving much of the day-to-day work to women.

eyes uncovered. At home, women engage in traditional activities, such as preparing meals for the family.

The increased use of the narcotic plant qat by men in some areas of the country has negatively affected the lives of many women. To provide for their families, some women work in the fields, as well as care for the home, while their husbands spend their days chewing qat and socializing.

Fathers usually arrange marriages for their daughters and, in return, receive money from the groom or his family. In some regions, arranged marriages have become similar to business deals in which men earn great amounts of money. In recent years, the government has tried to discourage this practice by limiting the amount of money men are allowed to of-

fer for a wife and by banning the marriage of girls under 16 years of age.

Health

Lack of money has limited the Yemeni government's ability to provide medical facilities and to train doctors. Rural clinics are especially understaffed. The country also has been too poor to develop adequate supplies of clean, drinkable water. Diseases caused by polluted water—including dysentery and schistosomiasis—are common. In addition, few children are vaccinated against measles and tuberculosis, both of which spread quickly among young Yemenis.

These conditions contribute to a high infant mortality rate. For every 1,000 live

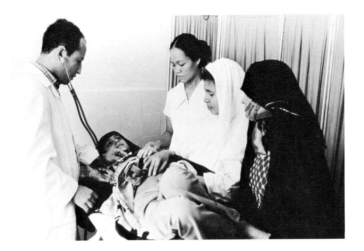

A doctor in Taizz examines a patient. Since the two Yemens joined, the government has focused on improving health care.

Nurse trainees in Sana listen to a lecture on nutrition.

births, 124 Yemeni babies die before they reach the age of one. Life expectancy at birth in Yemen is only 49 years—much lower than the rate in other countries on the Arabian Peninsula.

In recent years, the Yemeni government has increased its efforts to provide better health care. New hospitals have been built with foreign aid, and some rural health-care programs have begun operating. Officials have also established a new school of medicine at the University of Sana to train health-care workers.

Education and Language

For much of Yemen's history, education was available only to wealthy people. The majority of the population studied the Koran by reciting its prayers and rules but could not read or write. In the early 1990s, more than 80 percent of Yemeni adults were illiterate. The figure is higher among women, who until recently were not encouraged to seek schooling.

Yemen's new constitution states that all citizens have the right to an education. Public schools exist in large cities and towns. In many rural villages, children attend classes at Muslim religious schools. The University of Sana, which opened in 1970, offers courses in a variety of subjects, including history, science, math, economics, and law. Technical colleges and teacher-training institutes are located throughout the country.

The Yemeni government dedicates about 20 percent of its budget to education. Plans are under way to reduce the cost of primary education by replacing foreign teachers with Yemenis. Women are especially encouraged to enter the teaching profession. The government also plans to establish specialized schools for job training.

Arabic, Yemen's official language, is spoken throughout the country. Arabic has many different dialects that cannot always be mutually understood. Although spoken Arabic has evolved over time, the

Until the early 1990s, only one-fourth of all females in Yemen attended school. These Yemeni schoolgirls now have the opportunity to attend primary and secondary schools and to go on to college.

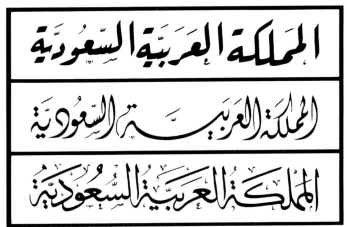

Arabic lettering appears in many styles. Thickly drawn characters *(top row)* are for everyday use. A more flowing form of the script *(middle row)* is used for special occasions. Very intricate writing *(bottom row)* appears in headlines and titles.

written language has not changed for hundreds of years. Arabic script is rounded and flowing, with connected characters written from right to left.

Some Yemeni students also learn English—the language of most foreign teachers. During Communist rule in the former PDRY, the Soviet Union helped to expand Yemen's industries and army. As a result, many Yemenis learned to speak Russian. Yemenis who have arrived from Ethiopia and other African nations use European and African languages.

The Arts

Yemen has a rich tradition of spoken literature. Nearly every village can trace

A Yemeni artisan stacks her pottery wares. In keeping with the teachings of the Koran, which forbids the depiction of living things, the pots are decorated with geometric designs.

A stained-glass artist shows off his work. Brightly colored stained glass is a popular art form that adorns many Yemeni homes.

its history and traditions through poetry and song. Local poets help to celebrate marriages or other occasions by creating verse on the spur of the moment. Traditional poetry is often broadcast on radio and television programs.

One of the most important books for Yemeni Muslims is the Koran, whose prayers and stories have been recited for centuries. The Koran forbids the depiction of living things on paintings and sculptures. To conform with these ideas, Muslims have developed complex geometric designs to decorate their mosques and houses. De-

tailed illustrations are also found in hand-decorated volumes of the Koran. Some modern artists have chosen to paint brightly colored landscapes and portraits despite Islamic rules.

Music accompanies Yemeni dancing and is an important part of festive occasions. In the cities, musicians play the *kabanj* (lute) and two small drums. In the Tihama, cymbals and violins accompany fast, intricate rhythms. In the highlands, musicians play a *mizmar* (a type of oboe) and beat a drum with their hands. The drummer often sings.

51

A jeweler in Sana shapes a new piece by hand. Yemen is famous for its beautiful silver jewelry.

Housing

Yemeni houses differ from region to region. In the coastal areas, dwellings display an African style, while houses in the highlands have a form unique to Yemen. Residents of the Hadhramaut build their homes with techniques from India, which greatly influenced Yemen during British rule.

In the Tihama, round or rectangular dwellings are made of mud-covered reeds and sticks. Many households consist of several one-room buildings, each of which serves a specific purpose. For example, a family might cook in one dwelling, entertain in a separate building, and sleep in yet another. Interior walls often feature painted scenes. Earthen walls or stone fences usually surround the reed homes of Tihama villages.

Yemenis in the highlands build stone and clay houses that are six or seven stories high. These houses are decorated with colored glass, carved wood, and alabaster. The stables and storage rooms occupy the lower levels. Several generations of one family usually share the upper levels, which contain living rooms, kitch-

Photo by Drs. A. A. M. van der Heyden, Naarden, the Netherlands

Residents of the highlands decorate their tower houses with white plaster in intricate designs.

ens, bathrooms, and one large room—called a *diwan*—that is used for celebrations. The owner of the house meets guests in an attic room called the *mafraj*.

In the wadis of eastern Yemen, villagers make their houses, mosques, and public wells with sun-dried bricks. These handmade clay bricks elaborately decorate the buildings' outside walls.

Courtesy of Hunt Oil Company/by Lynn Abercrombie

Many inhabitants of the Tihama live in circular dwellings made from mud, reeds, and sticks.

Food and Clothing

Yemen's fertile land and deep ocean waters provide the country's chief foods—rice, bread, vegetables, lamb, and fish. Yemenis eat a heavy midday meal that typically consists of chicken, lamb, or beef, accompanied by cooked vegetables and by rice mixed with raisins and almonds. Cooks cover a flat bread soaked in buttermilk with tomatoes, onions, and spices and serve a spicy green stew called *salta* at almost every meal. For dessert, Yemenis enjoy sweet custards with tea or spiced coffee.

Some Yemenis, especially those living in the cities, wear European-style clothing. Many others display traditional Arab dress. In the hot coastal regions, men wear a light-weight shirt, an embroidered skirt called a *futa*, and a straw hat or other head covering. In the colder highlands, a long shirt is worn with a jacket. Some men wear belts that hold a *jambiyya* (ceremonial dagger) that identifies their clan.

Women's styles vary from region to region. In Sana many women wrap themselves in bright cloths that are imported

Photo by Bernice K. Condit

At a dinner party, guests feast on a variety of traditional Yemeni dishes.

A Yemeni clansman tucks a traditional *jambiyya* (curved dagger) into his belt. The weapon, as well as the way he winds his headcloth, identifies the man's clan loyalties.

from India. In the Tihama, they wear colorful dresses and headdresses. Women from the Central Highlands sport baggy embroidered trousers called *sirwals* under their dresses. Women working in the fields of eastern Yemen dress in black robes and pointed straw hats. In keeping with Muslim rules, many women throughout Yemen cover themselves with long, black veils and capes.

In the Hadhramaut region, women cover themselves with long, black robes and wear straw hats for added protection from the sun.

A worker monitors the controls at an oil facility in central Yemen. The country's wells pump more than 300,000 barrels of oil per day.

4) The Economy

Throughout Yemen's history, agriculture has been an important economic activity. The Yemeni government wants to expand this sector, as well as to develop the transportation and communications systems needed to attract foreign companies.

Before unification, both Yemens depended heavily on foreign financial aid. The United States, Europe, and oil-rich Arab nations helped the YAR to build new roads, telephone lines, and hydroelectric power plants. After the 1967 revolution, PDRY leaders relied on aid from Communist countries. Unified Yemen still receives foreign assistance, but the country's op-

position to outside intervention during the Persian Gulf War was unpopular among Yemen's aid donors. Governmental officials believe that the recent discovery of oil in Yemen will boost the country's economy and lower its dependence on foreign funds.

Yemen's stance during the gulf war also contributed to soaring unemployment. In 1990, when Saudi Arabia expelled most Yemeni citizens, more than 700,000 jobless laborers returned to Yemen. The loss of money that the workers had been sending back to Yemen has hit many families hard. In addition, in 1992, thousands of refugees from Somalia—an African nation experiencing civil war and famine—entered Yemen, hoping to find food and jobs.

Agriculture and Fishing

Yemen contains some of the most fertile land on the Arabian Peninsula. As a result, the country has the potential to meet its own food needs and to export surplus crops. For this reason, agriculture has long been crucial to Yemen's economy. More than half the population are farmers.

Most farms are small and produce only enough crops to feed families or local communities. Although these holdings provide much of the country's food, some fruits and grains are imported. Yemen's hot climate supports drought-resistant crops, such as sorghum, millet, wheat, and barley. In eastern Yemen—where temperatures are warmer—bananas, dates, and grapes thrive along the wadis. Plans are under way to build new irrigation systems, which will increase the variety of crops that can be planted in Yemen.

Coffee, once Yemen's most profitable export, is now grown sparingly alongside qat in the highlands. Although qat claims more acreage and makes more money within the country, the leaves of this plant are considered a drug and cannot be exported legally. Farmers have planted qat on much of the land that once supported

Courtesy of FAO

After irrigating the land to loosen the soil, a farmer uses donkeys to plow his fields. Although Yemen has enough arable land to produce all its own food, imports have risen in recent years. A major goal for the new government is to restore self-sufficiency in agriculture.

A coffee grower near Ibb in southwestern Yemen examines his plants for ripe beans. Yemen was once one of the world's largest coffee producers, but farmers have replaced most of this crop with qat, a valuable domestic product.

food crops. The increased cultivation of qat has hurt Yemen's efforts to meet its own food needs.

Yemenis also breed livestock, such as sheep and goats, for their milk, meat, and hides. Until the mid-1980s, cattle, camels, and donkeys were raised for transportation. In recent years, farmers have begun to manage commercial chicken farms. In addition, some people keep bees to make

A fisherman strings his catch as other crews head toward shore.

Courtesy of FAO

Factory workers prepare freshly caught fish for drying. Although most fish is sold fresh in Yemen, some is dried for transport to the country's inland markets.

Yemeni honey, which is highly valued for its quality and taste.

One of the richest fishing areas in the world lies along Yemen's coast. Strong seasonal winds bring cool, nutrient-rich waters to the surface, causing plants and plankton to grow. As a result, a large variety of fish—such as tuna, mackerel, cod, red snapper, and lobster—feed in the area. Commercial boats, as well as small, independent fishing rigs, haul in large amounts of fish every year. Storage plants exist throughout Yemen, and canning factories operate in the coastal areas.

Oil and Mining

For decades, Yemen's Middle Eastern neighbors have exported huge quantities of oil from underground fields. In the early 1980s, the two Yemens explored their territories and found deposits of oil large enough for refining and for export.

The YAR quickly developed its oil resources with the help of U.S. companies. By 1986 five oil wells were pumping near Marib, and workers had laid a pipeline from the oil fields to the Red Sea. By 1989 the YAR was producing more than 200,000 barrels per day. The PDRY joined forces with a Soviet company in the late 1980s but still lacked the facilities to transport more than about 6,000 barrels daily. After the two Yemens united in 1990, a new pipeline was built and output increased to more than 120,000 barrels per day in the territory of the former PDRY.

To develop this valuable resource, the new government has signed contracts with foreign companies that hope to boost Yemen's oil production to 400,000 barrels per day. This figure will rank Yemen among the smaller producers in the Organization of Petroleum Exporting Countries (OPEC), a group of nations that regulates export of the fuel.

An oil pipeline stretches across the fertile fields of the Central Highlands.

Engineers have also found natural gas reserves in north central Yemen. This discovery has stimulated plans for construction of a gas-processing plant, gas-fired power stations, and a factory for bottling liquefied petroleum gas.

Yemeni mines and quarries produce salt, limestone, and marble. Some of the salt found along the Red Sea coast is used as a preservative for fish sent to inland markets, but most is exported. Limestone from the Tihama supplies the cement industry. Cement factories, however, do not produce enough to meet domestic needs. Marble has been quarried in Yemen since ancient times and remains one of the country's most important goods. Alabaster and pastel-tinted marble are in great demand for the construction of traditional buildings throughout the country.

The lights of an oil facility in central Yemen brighten the night sky. Oil production in Yemen is steadily increasing as new deposits are discovered.

A miner chips away at rock salt in a mine near Shabwa, the capital of the ancient Hadhramaut kingdom. Yemen also produces salt at coastal facilities, where workers flood enclosed areas with salty sea water. After evaporation, only the salt remains.

Photo by Lynn Abercrombie

Industry and Transportation

Before the revolutions of the 1960s, both Yemens largely depended on agriculture and fishing to earn money. Traditional industries included the manufacture of textiles, leather, baskets, jewelry, and glass. In recent years, Yemen has expanded its industrial base by building factories that manufacture soft drinks, cigarettes, aluminum, and food products.

Although a lack of skilled labor hampers expansion, new industries are operating in Yemen's major cities. In Aden, for exam-

ple, plans are under way to set up an industrial and commercial zone to encourage foreign investment. Increased oil revenues may also help to boost Yemen's sluggish manufacturing sector.

Yemen's poor transportation system has slowed the export of the country's goods. Buses and cars only recently replaced donkeys and camels as the main form of overland transportation. Since the early 1980s, workers have built a network of paved roads that now crosses the entire nation. In the highlands, however, the rugged terrain is a major obstacle to construction crews. The new government has made improvements in transportation a priority.

International flights can now enter Yemen through airports at Aden, Sana, Taizz, and Hodeida. The major airline—Yemen Airways—flies to Europe, Asia, and Africa, as well as to many cities within Yemen. The ports of Aden and Hodeida give access to major sea routes. Ships from many nations use the ports for refueling and repair. With improved roads, as well as sea and air links, Yemen has the potential to develop a profitable foreign trade.

The Future

The return of workers from Saudi Arabia has placed a great financial strain on Yemen. Although the new nation plans to expand industry, many of the returning laborers, as well as thousands of already unemployed workers, lack needed skills.

Government officials, who recognize that improved job training will help new industries succeed, have committed a large percentage of Yemen's annual budget to educating the country's work force.

Opposition to the presence of foreign forces in Saudi Arabia during the Persian Gulf War also harmed Yemen's relations with other countries. Highly dependent on outside aid, Yemen risks losing some of this funding. Determined to expand its oil industry, the Yemeni government hopes that profits from increased exports of oil will help to make up for the loss of foreign assistance.

Although some tensions remain among Yemeni clans, political parties, and religious groups, most citizens welcome unification. The government, which has broad public support, is working to modernize the new nation and to develop effective political and economic systems. If achieved, these improvements should benefit all Yemenis.

Independent Picture Service

The traditional Friday morning market opens in Amran, a village in northwestern Yemen. In recent years, this marketplace has greatly expanded, providing a boost to the town's economy.

Photo by Lynn Abercrombie

A pickup truck leaves a trail of deep ruts. Many roads in Yemen are unpaved, and some rugged mountain routes are impassable by automobile.

Index